BARRON'S

Thomas Haupt and Julie Rach Mancini

Cockatiels

Photographs: Karin Skogstad
Illustrations: György Jankovics

CONTENTS

THE TYPICAL
COCKATIEL

- Pointed crest a striking feature
- Gets along with others of its kind
- Friendly disposition; enjoys human company
- Black button eyes and delicate colors
- Enterprising and curious
- Slender shape
- Young stay in the nest until they fledge
- Easy to keep and to breed
- Loud voice that may take time getting used to

Its pleasant disposition, the ease with which it reproduces, and its simple requirements in captivity make the cockatiel an ideal "first bird," and it is in fact a favorite among aviculturists. Its adaptability and playfulness make it attractive not only to breeders but also to anyone simply wishing to have a pet bird. Cockatiels can also become good friends of children or companions of people who live alone.

6 DECISION MAKING

1 Cockatiels can live as long as 20 or 30 years. Are you ready to commit yourself for such a long time?

2 Bird cages and indoor aviaries are not cheap. Can you afford the purchase price and, more important, the ongoing costs for upkeep?

3 Cages have to be kept clean, food and water changed daily. Do you have time for these daily chores?

4 Cockatiels are sociable birds that live in flocks. Will you be able to satisfy your bird's need for daily contact and play?

6 Even though a cockatiel is a suitable pet for teaching children a sense of responsibility, an adult still has to check daily that the bird is properly cared for.

7 Do you have a place to take the bird to or a caretaker to look after it when you go away on vacation?

8 When your bird gets sick, you may have to take it to the veterinarian. Can your budget absorb extra costs for veterinarian's bills and medicines?

9 Do you already have pets that would not get along with a bird?

10 Is there a family member or anyone else living in your household who is allergic to feather dust, is bothered by noise, or doesn't like animals?

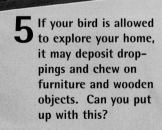

5 If your bird is allowed to explore your home, it may deposit droppings and chew on furniture and wooden objects. Can you put up with this?

One or Two Birds?

Cockatiels are extremely sociable and have a great need for social interaction. It is not always easy to satisfy this need, especially if you are not at home much. In this case, the best solution is to get two or more birds—assuming you have enough room for them.

A single bird gets more attached to its keeper than several kept together, but it does require a great deal of attention and affection from its keeper. If you can't spend time with your cockatiel every day, you should get at least two birds.

If you have a pair of birds, the female may lay eggs even if you had no intention of raising cockatiels. Should you consider breeding your birds, ask yourself before you go ahead whether you will be able to find homes for the offspring.

As a rule, two birds of the same sex (male or female) get along just as well as a mixed pair, especially if they were brought together while still young.

PREPARATION AND PURCHASE

With its tufted crest and black button eyes, a cockatiel is an impish-looking little bird that quickly charms its owners with its bright and cheerful ways. But for the bird to be happy in your home, certain criteria have to be met.

Origin

Cockatiels come from Australia, where they prefer open spaces, preferably near water. They are often found in areas where grain is grown. They live in pairs or small flocks, though when migrating or at water holes, up to 1,000 birds may come together.

When ranging across the continent in search of food, the birds depend on their excellent flying skills and endurance. They travel straight and fast, constantly utter loud cries while in the air to maintain contact, and land only to eat and drink. When on the ground they are very shy because of the danger of predators.

Cockatiels feed on the seeds of grasses and weeds, as well as on fruit and grain. If a flock alights on a wheat field, it may cause much damage, and farmers are, therefore, not very fond of the birds.

In Australia, cockatiels generally breed between August and December. Mating is triggered by the presence of sufficient food and water. As cavity breeders, cockatiels build their

Cockatiels are playful rascals. Appropriate toys keep them from getting bored.

nests in holes in old trees. Cockatiels do not display strict territorial behavior but defend only the immediate entry to their nest cavity against others of their kind. Consequently, several pairs can breed one above the other in cavities of the same tree.

Cockatiels as Pets

Nymphicus hollandicus—that's the cockatiel's scientific name—was first brought to Europe around 1840. In the early years collectors took young birds from their nests or caught entire flocks in order to satisfy the demand of zoos and bird fanciers for this parrot species. But on the long journey by boat, a great many birds perished, so people began to breed them in Europe.

Cockatiels were first successfully bred in Europe around 1850. Once the initial problem of providing appropriate nest sites was solved, breeding the birds became relatively easy. This was a good thing because in 1894 the Australian government imposed an export embargo on all native cockatiels. Today, the species is considered domesticated and is not subject to any regulations of species protection.

Where to Buy Cockatiels

Cockatiels are sold at pet stores, where you can usually choose from among a number of birds with different coloration (see page 12). You can also buy cockatiels from a serious breeder. You can get information on breeders from bird clubs or animal shelters. Any reputable pet dealer or responsible breeder will be knowledgeable and will try to offer only healthy birds in good condition. You should definitely buy a young bird if you expect it to become tame.

Cockatiels may also be available from bird rescue groups, which take in pet birds whose owners can no longer care for them. Check with your local animal shelters or do an online search to locate bird rescue groups in your area.

Things to Consider

Take plenty of time when buying your cockatiel and observe the various birds for sale carefully. Talk to the salesperson or breeder.

What you should watch for:
✔ If any birds exhibit signs of sickness, if their plumage is ruffled, or they sit apathetically in a corner, you should not buy them. The danger of acquiring a sick bird is too great.

Agile gymnasts, cockatiels make use of any opportunity to climb.

✔ Make sure everything is calm and quiet while you select your bird. Cockatiels are flock animals. If there is noise or a bustle in the room, all the birds, including the sick ones, will sit with their plumage pressed flat against the body so as not to reveal anything about their state to a possible enemy.
✔ All parrot species molt gradually. This means that the plumage is always complete and should be sleek, except when the birds are sleeping, in which case the feathers may be slightly puffed out. Sellers sometimes say that birds with bald spots or damaged plumage are molting, but in most cases these birds are sick.
✔ All parts that do not grow feathers—that is, beak, feet, and vent—should be smooth and without welts (danger of burrowing mites).
✔ The cages in which the birds for sale are kept should be large enough to accommodate the birds, clean, and with plenty of light.
✔ Do the birds have enough fresh food and water?
✔ Is there clean newspaper in the bottom of each cage?
✔ Watch the behavior of the birds. Are most of them sleeping? Are some of them very puffed up? Is the cage overcrowded?
✔ Do the birds have the possibility to satisfy, at least partially, their need for exercise and for flying, and do they make use of the opportunity?
All these observations and questions are

important in helping you decide whether or not to purchase a particular bird. If the pet store or breeder or the birds or their quarters seem questionable to you, don't buy in that establishment, not even out of pity. For the best start with your new pet, choose a healthy bird and take it to an avian veterinarian for a well-bird exam, especially if you have other birds in your home.

General Nature

Cockatiels can be very deliberate in their ways; they are not usually excitable birds. Their voices can be shrill, but content birds usually use this type of sound only to give out a warning noise when alarmed (or, in males, when performing a display of court-ship). More often, they use their voices for

Cockatiels are happiest when they are with others of their own kind.

whistling or for imitating words that they frequently hear.

Cockatiels can become lovable, tame, and trusting companions once they overcome their initial shyness and fear of entering new surroundings. They are usually content as long as they have things to work on with their beaks, such as branches, nibble sticks, or limestone blocks. Once you have the opportunity to observe your birds daily, you will become accustomed to their behavior patterns, their likes and dislikes, and you will see their personalities develop.

Choosing the Right Cockatiel

Signs that a cockatiel is healthy:
✔ Smooth plumage hugging the body.
✔ No breaks or bald spots in the plumage, even in juveniles. Fledglings leaving the nesting box are always fully feathered unless there is some health problem.
✔ Clear eyes free of discharge.
✔ No discharge from the nose.
✔ The vent is clean, without smears of feces.
Signs of illness:
✔ Subdued, apathetic behavior.
✔ Ruffled and disorderly plumage.
✔ Diarrhea.
✔ Sticky eyelids.
Never buy a cockatiel from a cage where there are sick birds because the infection may have spread to all the birds.

Male or Female?

If you want a cockatiel simply because you enjoy birds, the sex of the animal is not very important. Male and female birds become equally tame if you acquire them while they are young.

But if you care about the bird's ability to mimic and sing, you should get a cock, as the male birds are called. As part of their courtship behavior, with which they woo the chosen female, males often mimic sounds they hear. For more on the mimicking talent of cockatiels, see page 51.

Sexing cockatiels: If you intend to breed the birds, you obviously have to know their gender. Sexing cockatiels is difficult only in the case of juveniles, when males and females look almost identical. In older birds and those with the coloring of wild cockatiels, the sexes can be distinguished most easily by the shade of the mask, the area of the face that in males is set off conspicuously from the rest of the plumage. The mask of older males is yellow, that of females, pale yellow with a hint of gray. In juveniles the mask is still very muted. Both sexes have a red cheek spot, but in older males the red is brighter. Juveniles don't develop their facial coloring until they are eight or nine months old. Another difference is that in females the tail has horizontal yellow and black barring and the edges of the tail feathers are whitish; in males these feathers are gray.

If you are not sure about the sex of the bird you'd like to buy, ask the pet dealer or breeder.

Color Variants

In the course of captive breeding, cockatiels have been created in various colors that differ more or less markedly from those of the wild birds. Color mutations also occur in nature, but the oddly colored birds rarely survive and have little chance to pass on their genes. The situation is different in captivity. Here the breeder can select specific birds to bring out or eliminate certain traits in the offspring. When you buy a cockatiel, choose whatever color appeals to you. Color is no indication of a bird's character, talent, or disposition. The only thing to consider is that the sexes are harder to tell apart in some color strains than in others.

The following are the most common colors:
Normal: These birds are mostly gray. The breast and abdomen may be paler, and some individuals have a brownish tint. The crest and the mask (forehead and face) of the male are a bright yellow; in the female the mask is grayish. Both sexes have orange cheek or ear spots, which are more brightly colored in the male.

The outer tail feathers are yellow in the female but with pronounced dark gray marbling. Young birds resemble the female except that the males have more yellow feathers in the head area. Juveniles acquire their adult plumage at about eight months.

Lutinos: In this type, all pigmentation except yellow is eliminated, and the birds therefore appear yellowish. They are not albinos because some color pigments are left, but, like albinos, these birds have red eyes. The pairing of Lutinos has led to the bald spot on the back of the head typical of this strain, which may be passed on to other color variants. The gene for Lutino coloring is linked to the sex chromosome, which means that these hereditary traits show up only in certain birds, depending on the sex of the parent carrying the trait.

Fruits and vegetables are essential ingredients of a balanced diet.

Pied: The appearance of this type is quite varied. Pieds have white or yellow patches of various size all over the body. There are also Pieds in different color combinations.

Cinnamons: This type probably originated in Belgium. The gray color of these birds is lighter than that of the Normal, and the entire body has a delicate cinnamon hue. The other parts of the plumage are like those of the Normal. The nestlings have red eyes, but the eye color changes over time. This color variation, too, is sex-linked.

Pearl: This type was first bred in Germany around 1967. In these birds the feathers on the back, throat, breast, and rump are gray with light edges; or are light colored with dark edges. This gives them a kind of fish-scale appearance. The crest is dark. While young, the males resemble female birds, but as they grow up, the pearled look disappears, and as adults they look like Normal cockatiels. Birds whose light-colored feathers are bright yellow are called Golden Pearls.

Silver: This type is a light gray with what looks like a dusting of silver. These birds have red eyes. They are almost indistinguishable from light-colored Normal cockatiels.

Caution: Because of a lethal gene, some offspring of two Silver parents die while still in the egg.

White-faced: This type has no yellow or orange whatsoever at any age. The mask of the male, therefore, is pure white. The head of the female is a light gray. Even the down feathers of the nestlings are white. This mutation first appeared in Europe around 1978.

Albinos: This type lacks all pigment and is therefore pure white with red eyes. The beak and claws are also whitish. This variant resulted from the crossing of White-faced and Lutino birds.

Breeders can combine color strains to create multiple color variations in the same bird. Other colors you may encounter include Fallow, Emerald, Platinum, Yellow-Cheeked, Pastel, and Cinnamon White-Faced.

PORTRAITS:
COCKATIELS

Cockatiels are bred in many different color variations, but there is no connection between the shade of the plumage and a bird's temperament and behavior.

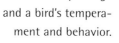

Right: A Normal male in full adult plumage.

Left: A Pearl cockatiel contemplating an apple.

Left, below: The Pearl cockatiel is inviting the Pied bird to scratch its neck.

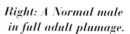

Above: A Lutino busy with a spray of millet.

Below: Two Pieds peacefully eating a spray of millet.

Above: A Lutino and a Pied female fighting over a spray of millet.

Left: A gorgeous Pied.

Above: A Normal at left and a Pearl at right.

Left: A Lutino at left and a Normal at right.

Housing and Supplies

You should set up the cage for your cockatiel before you go out to get the bird. This will help ease the bird's transition into your home because it will be able to move into its new cage as soon as you bring it home, instead of having to wait in its travel carrier while you set up its cage.

Types of Cages

When you visit a pet store or look through bird magazines, you will notice two main types of cages: wire and acrylic. Bird cages have traditionally been made of wire, and wire works quite well for most bird owners. Most bird owners will select a wire cage, but let's look briefly at the benefits of an acrylic cage before you make a final decision.

Acrylic cages have been widely available since the mid-1990s. Their main benefit is in

mess containment. Since there are no bar spaces in an acrylic cage, seed hulls, loose feathers, and other debris stay within the cage and fall into the cage tray for easy removal. Stuck-on food or droppings clean off the cage walls easily with a damp paper towel, which is another advantage when it comes time to clean the cage.

If you select an acrylic cage for your cockatiel, set it up out of direct sunlight because birds in acrylic cages may be more prone to overheating than those kept in wire cages. Also, make sure the cage has plenty of ventilation holes drilled in it for maximum air circulation.

If you select a wire cage for your pet (as most bird owners do), keep in mind that bar spacing is an important factor in cage selection. You don't want the bars to be far enough apart that your bird can get its head caught between them or that it can escape through the bars. Recommended bar spacing in a cockatiel cage is about $1/2$ inch (12.7 mm). The cage should also have both vertical and horizontal bars in it so your pet can climb around the cage to exercise.

Size

We can give you only a minimum size. A cage should be no smaller than 24 × 16 × 24 inches (60 × 40 × 60 cm) for a single bird. The rule of thumb is that your bird has to be able to spread out both wings without touching anything and that the tail should not constantly brush against the cage bars. The perches should therefore not be located too close to the side walls. The height of the perches is secondary, but be sure the bird can always sit upright.

Spreading the wings and tail aids relaxation.

Cage decorations are generally of no practical use and just get in the way. Their appeal is limited to the owner; to the cockatiel they serve no purpose.

Shape

The floor plan of the cage should be rectangular. Round cages ought to be relegated to museums. Because the bars of round cages are vertical the bird can't make use of them for climbing, and because of their small diameter, these cages don't offer enough room for movement.

The cage should have at least two doors, and fairly large ones, so you can clean the cage and perform other necessary chores

The horizontal bars of the cage provide opportunity for climbing.

without having to bend and twist uncomfortably. Even the danger of escape doesn't justify small doors.

Clean-out drawers should slide in and out smoothly.

A large cage should be placed on a stand with rollers. This makes maintenance easier and also allows you to move the bird to a window or onto the balcony for a change of scenery. You do, however, have to be careful not to expose the bird to drafts or to direct sunlight that it can't get away from.

...e thick enough so that the ...n't reach all the way around them. ...erches help wear down the claws so ...at they don't grow too long. Natural sticks and branches are best because their irregularities provide a kind of massage for the feet. The birds also like to nibble on the bark, which supplies them with some minerals and gives them something to do.

Branches of conifers, though not poisonous, are not acceptable because they tend to be very resinous. The resin can get the feathers sticky, and if it gets into the digestive tract it can lead to death.

The right number of perches is also important for the well-being of a cockatiel. If there are too many, they interfere with the bird's movements. The best arrangement is to have one perch in the upper part of the cage, a second one somewhat lower, and a third one still a little higher.

The space between the perches should be large enough so that the bird's tail doesn't constantly rub against a lower perch. This damages the feathers.

Don't place the perches too low. Birds like to sit high up in order to have a good view of their surroundings. The only low perches should be in front of the food dishes.

Food tastes best if it's shared with a friend.

Food Dishes

Get at least three dishes: one for dry food, one for fruit and sprouts, and one for water. The dishes can be of metal, hard plastic, or china. What is important is that they be the right size and easy to clean. It is essential to check and replenish food and water dishes daily.

Automatic food dispensers are not recommended for cockatiels because they can get clogged. They give the false sense that the bird has plenty of food when it may in fact be unable to get at fresh seeds.

Lining the Cage

Line your bird's cage tray with black-and-white newspaper, used computer paper, or white paper towels. These are the easiest cage liners to use, and they are also the safest in case your bird nibbles on the cage liner.

To keep your pet out of the cage tray, purchase a cage with a built-in grille. The grille prevents your cockatiel from getting into its discarded food and droppings, which can help keep it healthier.

Do not line your bird's cage with grit, sand, walnut shells, or ground corncobs. These can all cause health problems for your cockatiel. Also, do not use sandpaper cage covers on the perches to protect your bird from foot problems later on.

Toys

Give your cockatiel unbreakable objects made of metal or hardwood to play with.

Toys made of sisal are dangerous because the bird may get entangled in the fibers, or if the bird eats some of the sisal, it may develop inflammation of the crop or digestive problems.

Important: Even if your cockatiel has a large and well laid-out cage, your bird must be able to spend some time outside of it. Cockatiels need lots of exercise, which they can get only if they can spend time outside their cages on a play gym.

Placement of the Cage

When your bird first arrives in its new home, the cage or indoor aviary should already be placed where it is going to stay permanently.

✔ The cage should be near a window. This way the bird can watch what is going on outside, it is exposed to the natural rhythm of day and night, and it has a chance to get some sun. However, the bird must always be able to retreat to the shade.

✔ The cage should not be too low because birds must be able to survey the world around them. Eye level with people is about the right height.

✔ Put the cage where you spend much of your time; otherwise, the bird will be lonely and will fail to get attached to you.

✔ There should be no heater or radiator nearby. Rising hot air dries out a bird's mucous membranes and can lead to illness.

✔ Smoke is harmful to birds.

Checklist
Cage and Equipment

1 A metal or acrylic cage with sufficiently large doors, an unbreakable bath, and a clean-out drawer.

2 If you are buying only one cockatiel but are considering adding another, the cage should be no smaller than 40 × 28 × 51 inches (100 × 70 × 130 cm).

3 Cage bars should be primarily vertical and spaced $1/2$ of an inch (1.25 cm) apart.

4 Perches of hardwood dowels or branches of unsprayed fruit trees, shrubs, willows, poplars, or nut trees.

5 At least three food dishes of metal, hard plastic, or china, for water, dry food, and fruit and sprouts.

6 Appropriate chew toys designed for cockatiels.

7 A spray bottle to give the cockatiel showers.

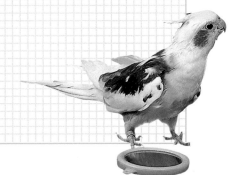

The Trip Home

You will be handed your cockatiel in a travel box especially designed so that the bird will not hurt itself and will stay calm. This box will later come in handy for trips to the veterinarian. Take the bird home without making stops along the way. When you get there, hold the open box up to the cage, which you will have prepared for its occupant beforehand, and wait until the cockatiel climbs through the cage door. You

This cockatiel is obviously happy to be near a window.

may have to wait several minutes. Then go away; the bird should not be bothered the first day in its new home.

Winning the Bird's Trust

The first few days are usually the most difficult. Do the necessary caretaking chores quietly and always in the same way. That makes the process less threatening.

If your cockatiel is very shy, sit down at some distance from the cage and talk to the bird in a soft, reassuring tone.

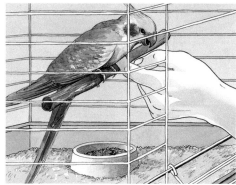

By moving your hand slowly toward the bird's abdomen, you will gradually win your bird's trust.

Hand-taming a Cockatiel

✔ Gradually move closer to the cage when you talk to the bird.
✔ When your cockatiel is accustomed enough to you that you can stand next to the cage, put your hand against the bars, but not above the bird; otherwise, the bird might think a predator is approaching from above.

✔ Slowly reach inside the cage and extend your hand toward the bird.
✔ When your hand is very close to the bird, start stroking its head gently. Offering a treat at the same time may do wonders.
✔ Move your hand to the bird's abdomen from below and push up a little. The bird will often respond by climbing onto your hand.
✔ Practice this until the cockatiel always climbs onto your hand when you encourage it to do so.
✔ Don't take the bird out of the cage until the bird consistently climbs onto your hand. Avoid abrupt movements.

This is how your cockatiel learns to climb onto your finger.

Night Rest

As a rule, cockatiels follow an inborn schedule of rest and wakefulness, which you should respect. But the birds are also flexible and will often adjust to your daily life rhythm. It is important, however, that their night rest be undisturbed.

When a cockatiel gets ready to retire, it settles down on its sleeping perch. At this point it should be left undisturbed. To prevent the bird from waking up at night startled, flying up, and possibly hurting itself,

Undisturbed sleep is important for the bird's health.

you can leave on a small night light (10 or 20 watt).

Cover the cage with a cloth. This gives the bird the feeling of security at bedtime.

Minor squabbling over treats is nothing to worry about, but if a real fight develops, you have to separate the birds.

Getting Two Birds Used to Each Other

If you already have one cockatiel and then get a second one, or if you have bought two, you should be present for the first few hours the birds spend together in order to prevent fights or accidents. Although cockatiels usually get along well together, problems may arise. The established bird often takes a few days before it accepts the new partner.

If the cage or aviary is quite large, you can place both birds in it and watch them. If there is only minor bickering but no real fighting in the first few hours, things usually continue peacefully. But if the birds attack each other you have to separate them.

Keep the birds in separate cages next to each other. After a while they can be brought together on neutral ground, perhaps in the room. If all goes well, both birds can be put in one cage.

For the health of the first bird, quarantine all new arrivals for at least 60 days in a separate room to ensure that the new bird isn't sick.

DAILY MANAGEMENT AND CARE

Once your cockatiel has overcome its fear of you and climbs onto your hand, you will start having a wonderful time with it. But in order to offer it a full and happy life, you have to make sure you respect its natural needs, feed it a healthy and varied diet, and take good care of it.

Taking Care of Your Cockatiel

Your cockatiel has a few daily care requirements that are easy to manage. It needs pellets and a variety of fresh foods and clean water, all served in clean dishes, and it needs to have the cage paper changed. You should also look at the cage and at your bird to see that it hasn't injured itself somehow and that it seems content and healthy. Notice the food and water levels as you service your pet's cage to ensure that it's eating and drinking normally. If it isn't, contact your avian veterinarian's office for an evaluation appointment. Spend a little time in the morning and in the evening talking to your pet, and give it plenty of cuddles and head scratches. Also, be sure to take it out of its cage for some supervised playtime with you or on its playgym.

✔ Wipe down the cage bars with a damp sponge daily and scrape off any large droppings

Cockatiels like to nibble on plants. Make sure there are no poisonous ones around.

as soon as you can so that they don't become stuck on the bars.

✔ Once a week, you will need to wash and disinfect your cockatiel's cage to protect it from illness. Remove the bird from the cage and house it in its travel carrier. Empty the cage tray and slide it back into place at the bottom of the cage. Take all other items (toys, perches, and bowls) out of the cage, and let the bowls and perches soak in hot water.

✔ Place the empty cage and tray into the shower and let hot water run over it to loosen any stuck-on food or droppings. Scrub the cage and tray with a stiff-bristled brush to remove any debris, and rinse with hot water. Spray the cage and tray with a bird-safe disinfectant and allow it to stay on the cage as directed by the product instructions. Rinse the cage and tray thoroughly and dry them completely before relining the tray with fresh paper and replacing your bird in its home.

✔ Wash the dishes and perches with hot, soapy water and rinse them completely, too. Allow the dishes to air-dry, and dry wooden perches in a 400°F (185°C) oven for 10 minutes before returning them to the cage. Provide fresh food and water for your bird and replace

Poisonous and Dangerous Plants

Cockatiels like to nibble on plants; unfortunately, they cannot tell poisonous from harmless ones. That's why it's up to you to make sure that there are no dangerous plants or substances that could make the bird sick anywhere where it might get at them.

House and garden plants considered poisonous:

Euphorbia species, Dieffenbachia, crown-of-thorn, yew, hyacinth, periwinkle, deadly nightshade, poinsettia, narcissus, oleander, Ardisia, four-o'clock, maidenhead fern.

Considered extremely dangerous:

Ivy, philodendron, flamingo flower (*Anthurium*), golden trumpet *(Allamanda cathartica)*, resinous woods, *Schefflera*.

With cacti, special caution is in order because of their spines. Young birds are especially likely to get hurt because they are still inexperienced and clumsy.

Before buying a new plant, ask if it might be harmful to birds. Better to do without the plant than take a chance with your cockatiel's well-being.

A local garden center, a county extension office, or an avian veterinarian can help determine if specific plants are safe.

its perches. Inspect toys for signs of wear before putting them back into your bird's cage, and rotate the toys regularly to provide your bird with new and interesting opportunities to play.

Grooming

Another important part of regular bird care is grooming your cockatiel's wings and nails. See the "How-To" section on page 38 for more information on how to help keep your bird safe by keeping its wing feathers and nails trimmed. Cockatiels need to have their wings trimmed at least four times a year, so keep an eye on feather length. If your bird suddenly takes wing inside your home, it's time for a trim. Cockatiels are strong, swift flyers, so it's important to keep feathers trimmed to prevent your pet from flying away from home.

Stepping Up and Down

Get your bird accustomed to stepping up and down on your hand so that you can safely carry it from place to place. Offer your finger in front of your bird at the same level as its feet and say "*Step up*" as you gently push your finger into the bird's belly. The bird will soon understand what you want it to do and will follow your command. Praise the bird for behaving as you want it to, and offer head scratches or a favorite food treat to further encourage good behavior. To have the bird step down, hold your hand (with the bird on it) near a perch in its cage and say "*Step down*" as you guide the bird toward the perch and off your hand. Reward good behavior as outlined above, and your bird will soon be stepping up and down with confidence!

Don't allow your bird to sit on a door because its toes can get pinched when the door closes.

Avoiding Dangers

Source of Danger	Danger	Avoiding the Danger
Open doors	Flying into rooms not meant for the bird	Keep doors closed to all rooms where bird is not supposed to fly
Other pets in the home	Bird is stepped on or bitten by other pets	Keep bird away from other pets
Clothes lying on floor	Bird crawls under them and may get hurt	Get used to walking gingerly; don't leave things lying around
Containers with water	Bird may slip in and drown	Always watch the bird; if necessary, cover container
Open closets and drawers	Bird is closed in by mistake	Always keep closets and drawers closed or check them frequently
Poisons such as alcohol, magic markers, salt, verdigris, solvents, fertilizers, cleansers, lead weights in drapes	Poisoning by ingestion	Keep poisonous substances in inaccessible places; don't offer alcohol, even as a joke at parties
Stove burners, hot irons, candles, fireplace, nonstick cooking surfaces	Burns, possibly fatal; poisoning by inhalation	Always keep bird in cage when you cook or iron or have an open fire; avoid airborne toxins
Waste basket, decorative vases	Bird slips in and is unable to climb out again	Woven baskets are easier to climb out of; filling vessels with sand prevents bird from falling in; cover vessels while bird is flying free
Direct sun for prolonged period	Heatstroke and heart attack	Place cage so bird can choose to be in sun or shade
Stoves, electrical appliances	Burns, fatal electric shock if bird chews on wires	Put appliances where bird can't get at them; cover securely
Extreme temperature fluctuations	Colds, pneumonia, heatstroke, freezing to death	Gradually acclimatize bird to changes in temperature

10 Golden Rules
on Proper Care

1 If you want to make sure from the beginning that you'll have a happy bird, get two cockatiels.

2 In all your dealings with the bird, act quietly and calmly; a hectic pace makes any bird nervous.

3 Get the cockatiel used to your hand. Always raise your hand toward its abdomen from below and encourage the bird to step onto it.

4 Never leave children under the age of 12 alone with the bird so that both parties are safe from accidents.

5 Don't approach your cockatiel unexpectedly with quick movements; this would scare it.

6 Regular exercise periods are important; they keep your bird healthy and in good shape, and they provide entertainment.

7 A cockatiel cannot be house-trained. Knowing this, take appropriate measures, such as spreading newspapers on the floor.

8 Rearrange the inside of the cage periodically and offer food in new places. That keeps the bird alert.

9 Variety in the composition of the bird's diet is important; so is a regular feeding schedule, which will help you to not forget anything.

10 Clean the cage and everything in it regularly to prevent disease, and disinfect the cage completely each week. Use a bird-safe product and rinse the cage and accessories completely before returning the bird to the cage.

A Bird-proof Room

To make sure your bird is safe when flying you have to take some precautions.

✔ Check that all windows in the room are completely shut. Your bird would not be the first to escape through a cracked window. You may want to put up screens so that fresh air can still enter the room, which is important for your bird.

✔ Pull the curtains or lower the shades. Birds don't know about glass and will try to fly through what looks to them like an opening. Crashing against a window can cause serious injury and even death. You can gradually open the curtains or shades a couple of inches a day, to get the bird used to the glass.

✔ Bureaus and cupboards have to be shoved up against the wall so the cockatiel can't slip behind them and be unable to get out again on its own.

✔ Don't leave filled flower vases or watering cans standing around; if the cockatiel peers in to see what's there, it may slip in and drown.

✔ Birds like to chew on electric wires—with possibly fatal results. If you can, run the wires behind furniture or under rugs, or run them through a metal pipe.

✔ Keep no poisonous plants or objects made of pewter or lead in the room. The bird might nibble on them. Many substances are toxic for birds, among them sprays, diuretics, mercury, plastic film and bags, glues, varnish, spices, and ballpoint pen cartridges.

What to Do if the Bird Escapes

Cockatiels are swift flyers that can develop speed even inside a room, so if you don't watch, even for a minute, your bird might get away.

In the summer the bird may survive in the wild for a time as long as it doesn't fall victim

These two birds are about to enjoy some time outside their cage.

to a predator, fly into a power line, or get hit by a car. It will find seeds, fruit, and berries to eat. This is not so in winter when it may manage for a while by joining a flock of wild birds and visiting bird feeders. The cold is not that serious, but in the long run, a cockatiel will not survive on its own.

The bird may luck out if hunger or tameness drives it to seek out people. If that happens, the ring on its foot makes it possible to find the rightful owner.

If your cockatiel has escaped but is still close by, place its cage with food in it outside and hope the bird will find its way back into it. If the bird has settled on a tree that is not too tall, you can aim a strong spray of water at it; a bird can't fly if its plumage is soaked. But you have to do it quickly; if the bird gets scared before it is immobilized, it will disappear for good.

VACATION PLANS

Vacation time raises the question of what to do with the bird.

In some cases, you can take your bird along on the trip, while in others, you will have to board the bird or arrange for a pet-sitter to care for your cockatiel in your home.

✔ *If you are not going a great distance, you can take your bird along in a smaller travel cage. Don't expose it to drafts, heat, or full sun on the way. Protect your pet from heatstroke by never leaving it in a car on a warm day.*

✔ *Find a place where you can board your bird. Ask at your pet store, local animal shelter, or veterinarian. Or perhaps a friend or relative is willing to take in your bird. An even better solution is if the vacation caretaker can stay in your house or apartment and look after the bird in its familiar surroundings.*

✔ *Make preparations for your absence way ahead of time. Write up a sheet with directions, including important addresses and where you can be reached, and leave it with the caretaker.*

In the wild, cockatiels behave in a way you can make use of when attempting to retrieve your bird. A pair of cockatiels will try to keep in contact with each other by calling constantly if one partner is not close by. Sometimes, the bird that stays behind lures its runaway mate back to the cage with its calls.

Here are some other things to do when recovering an escaped bird:

• Keep the bird in sight.
• Play a recording of your bird's voice to bring it home.
• Call veterinary offices and your local humane society to let them know you've lost a bird.
• Put up fliers. Offer a reward and include your phone number.

Cockatiels and Children

Cockatiels are not ideal pets for children, especially for very young ones. They don't like to be petted and cuddled, and children's hands may unintentionally be too rough for the small feathered body.

If your child insists on a bird, keep in mind that a cockatiel needs not only affection but also proper care and things to occupy it. Also, remember that keeping a bird costs money, though not vast sums.

For maximum enjoyment by all family members, keep the cockatiel as a family pet. Encourage your children to participate in its daily care and provide them with backup to ensure that the bird isn't left in a dirty cage without fresh food and water. Many children quickly lose interest in a pet bird, but some become faithful caretakers with a little encouragement.

If your child is truly interested in keeping birds, especially small parrots, a cockatiel is—along with the budgerigar—the most perfect first bird because its care is relatively simple and it becomes tame quite quickly. Thus, a close friendship between child and bird can develop that lasts for years, while the child learns to take responsibility for another creature.

Cockatiels and Other Pets

Although it may seem like a good idea to combine cockatiels with other small parrots or songbirds in a mixed aviary, it's better to keep cockatiels to themselves. Some cockatiels have been known to act aggressively toward other smaller birds, such as finches, canaries, or lovebirds, and keep them away from food and water sources. Don't try to house cockatiels with other small parrots in a large cage, either, because the same problems could result.

Dogs, unless they have a pronounced hunting instinct, generally show little interest in cockatiels, but you should never leave the two animals alone together, even if you are at home. Big dogs can sometimes seriously hurt a bird without intending to, simply because of their clumsiness.

Cats are more problematic because they are hunters by nature. A relatively peaceful coexistence can be achieved if the cockatiel learns from the beginning to defend itself with its beak whenever the cat gets too close. But this generally works only if the cat is introduced to the bird as a kitten. Even in that case, never leave the cat and bird alone together. The cat might pounce during a moment of inattention on the part of the bird.

Always keep in mind that many cockatiels are docile birds. Almost any larger-sized parrot, and even most smaller ones, may be more aggressive than your cockatiel. You may find that it is better to avoid introductions with other animals in order to ensure that your cockatiel is safe. As with other predatory pets such as ferrets, snakes, and certain lizards, as well as dogs and cats, maintaining a "separate but equal" policy in your household may be helpful. Each animal will get some of your attention, just not at the same time.

Mutual interest in each other can be the beginning of a long-lasting friendship.

The Proper Diet

Pet stores sell ready-made seed mixtures for cockatiels that resemble what the birds would eat in the wild.

A seed mixture should consist of small seeds, such as various kinds of millet, canary seed, and canola seed. Larger seeds, such as hulled oats, wheat berries, buckwheat, hemp seed, and safflower seed are added. Sunflower seeds and nuts should be given only sparingly because they are high in fat and may lead to obesity. They also satisfy a bird's appetite too quickly. By contrast, small seeds are high in carbohydrates and stimulate intestinal activity, and, because they are small, the cockatiel has to eat

Rowanberries add variety to the diet, and this female seems to find them tasty.

more of them, which keeps the bird occupied and entertained.

Freshness of the food is especially important. The older seeds or grain are, the less their nutritional value. A good way to check the freshness is to test for viability. Try sprouting a sample every so often (see page 32).

Spoiled food threatens the health of your cockatiel.

✔ Seeds high in fat, such as hemp and sunflower seeds, can get rancid.

✔ You can tell mildew by the whitish gray coating on the seeds and a sharp smell.

✔ Rotten food also smells bad and is slimy to the touch.

✔ Although meal moths are harmless, don't feed infested seeds to your birds. Infested seeds have a "webby" appearance in which the grains are clumped together.

The basic rule is to store birdseed in an airy, dry place, or keep it in the refrigerator.

Spray millet is an easily digestible treat that young or sick birds enjoy particularly. It is also an important supplement to the diet for breeding pairs. A healthy cockatiel should get at most about 2 inches (5 cm) a day.

Seeds glued to heart or ring shapes with honey help keep a bird occupied, but they are loaded with calories. Fresh branches the bird can nibble on serve the same purpose much better.

Drinking water: You can simply use the water from your tap, or you can buy uncarbonated mineral water low in sodium. The water dish must be cleaned and refilled every day.

The Right Amount of Food

✔ The basic guideline is one to two tablespoons of seed per bird per day.

✔ Since birds have a high rate of metabolism and low stores of energy, it is important for them to eat small amounts frequently.

✔ To be on the safe side, always give a little more than the required daily ration.

✔ Empty and wash the seed dish before adding new seeds.

Important: Don't try to keep your bird at an optimal weight by limiting its food intake. In case of illness, the body's metabolism speeds up, and the bird needs more energy. If it can't get it by eating more, its state of health will rapidly decline. It is better to control weight by providing for more exercise.

Checklist
Feeding Rules

1 Feed the bird daily and, if possible, always at the same time.

2 Always give a little more food than necessary. However, there is no need for heaping dishes or more than one dish for the same food.

3 Fruits, vegetables, and greens should be given daily and must always be fresh. Put them in a separate dish. You may mix fruit in with wet food or sprouts.

4 Always wash and preferably peel fruit that is not from your own garden or from a farm you know; then let the water drip off.

5 Regularly offer fresh branches, nibble sticks, or a limestone block. The nibble sticks to which seeds are glued with honey are high in calories. Give them only rarely.

6 Offer food, especially treats, frequently from your hand. This encourages the cockatiel to become tame.

TIP

Scraps from the Table

Not suitable:
✔ Pretzels and chips because too much salt and fat are bad for liver and kidneys.
✔ Chocolate, candy, and cookies have too much fat, sugar, and artificial coloring.
✔ Alcohol and coffee.
Acceptable:
✔ Fruit juice containing no sugar.
✔ Dry bread, whole wheat crackers, whole grain breakfast cereals.
✔ Cooked potatoes and pasta, but not too hot.
✔ Lean meat.
✔ Occasionally yogurt, low-fat cottage cheese, or a very small amount of mild cheese.
✔ Black tea but only for a short time as an emergency measure against diarrhea.

Preparing Sprouts

Making sprouts takes a little extra time but has many advantages.
✔ Sprouts have more vitamins than other foods and are more easily digested.
✔ The swelling and sprouting process opens up the seeds and increases the vitamins and other nutrients contained in them.
✔ For young birds, sprouted seeds are easier to hull and eat.

To soak seeds, place them in a small bowl (you can use your commercial seed mixture, perhaps adding some corn, beans, peas, and oats) and cover them with water. After 12 hours rinse the seeds well. You can now mix in some fruit, add some egg food (available at pet

stores), and give the food to your cockatiel.

To sprout seeds, you have to soak the swelled seeds again and rinse them again after 12 hours. Then you put them in a sieve placed in a dish and cover with a plate so they won't dry out. Let the seeds stand at room temperature another 24 to 48 hours, until they have started to sprout. If you want to give your bird sprouts every day, you will have to start several batches, one a day. Seeds that have gotten too dry don't sprout well, but they can be given just soaked.

Refrigerate sprouted seeds to maintain their freshness, and rinse them thoroughly before offering them to your cockatiel. Remove sprouted seeds within a few hours of offering them to protect your bird from eating spoiled food. Discard any sprouts that look or smell rotten before giving them to your bird.

Fruits and Vegetables

You can offer your bird just about any fruits and vegetables except cabbage, potatoes, avocados, and citrus fruit. In addition, you can give herbs and wild greens, such as basil, parsley, chervil, meadow grass, cow vetch, dandelion (leaves and stalks), sorrel, shepherd's purse, and watercress.

What is important is that the plants be unsprayed. If you buy fruits or vegetables, wash them thoroughly and, where appropriate, peel.

Keep in mind when feeding:
✔ Offer plenty of variety.
✔ If a bird refuses a particular food, keep offering it nevertheless.
✔ The chunks should not be too big; the cockatiel must be able to move them with its tongue.
✔ Pieces that are too small lose their texture quickly and get mushy.
✔ Offer fruits and vegetables in a separate dish or combined with soaked or sprouted

seeds, but the bird always has to have a separate dish with dry seeds available as well.

✔ Do not feed cabbage and raw potatoes to your bird.

✔ Watch out with lettuce. Because of its high water content, lettuce may contain traces of many pesticides. If you grow your own lettuce organically you can give small amounts of it without worrying.

✔ Fasten greens to the cage bars with a clothespin (not the spring type).

Vitamins

Since there is no way of knowing how many vitamins your bird gets in its fresh food, you should add vitamins to its diet several times a week. You can do this by sprinkling a powdered supplement on its fresh foods. Ask your veterinarian to recommend a good vitamin supplement for birds.

In the past, bird owners used to add vitamins to their birds' drinking water, but this practice is now discouraged. Vitamins in the water may change its taste, and this may make a bird less likely to drink an adequate amount of water. Also, bacteria can grow quickly in water that has been enriched with vitamins.

Minerals and Trace Elements

These substances are necessary to maintain strong bones and a healthy plumage; young birds need them for growth, and females for egg production. Some minerals are present in

the food but others have to be added. When you buy mineral powder, make sure that it contains the substances necessary for skeletal growth and the formation of feathers; this information should appear on the product's label.

In nature, birds absorb minerals by eating some earth. As a substitute you should give your cockatiel bird grit. This is a mixture of different kinds of rock, seashells, oyster shells, cuttlefish, and limestone. You can also buy a mineral powder that you mix in the bird's food.

Food Pellets

Cockatiels were among the first pet birds to eat a pelleted diet when a researcher in California began developing his pelleted diets by feeding them to a flock of cockatiels in the 1980s.

Pellets contain all the nutrients a bird needs in the right amounts, but since eating them requires no work, some birds may become bored with them. You can solve this problem before it starts by offering pellets along with a variety of fresh foods that your bird has to work at in order to eat, such as peas in the pod or a slice of corn on the cob.

Fruits and vegetables are an important source of vitamins for cockatiels.

Information on Breeding

Cockatiels are ideal birds with which to begin a breeding operation. Pairs go to nest readily and are usually good parents, producing several clutches a year. Ideally, you should remove the nest box and let the parent birds rest after they've raised two clutches in a year. This will help them maintain their health for the following year's breeding cycle.

The Breeding Cage

Cockatiels are relatively easy to breed and can be raised in almost any kind of cage, but it should be large enough to accommodate not only the nest box but for a while, the young birds as well. The larger the cage, the better. An aviary would be ideal.

If you mount the nest box so it hangs outside the cage, the birds have some extra room and you will also find it easier to do the necessary nest checking.

Nest boxes are sold in two shapes, tall and squat. In the tall ones, the floor area should be 10 × 12 × 12 inches (26 × 30 × 30 cm), and the walls should be 13 to 15 inches (33 to 38 cm) high. The squat ones measure about 12 × 16 inches (30 × 40 cm) and are 10 inches (25 cm) high. The bottom board should have a thickness of 1⅜ inches (3.5 cm); the side walls can be thinner.

For all types of nest boxes:
✔ The entry hole has to have a diameter of 3⅛ to 3½ inches (8 to 9 cm).
✔ Put a layer of wood shavings in the bottom of the box as nesting material.
✔ Since many females remove the litter, it is a good idea to carve a hollow in the floor of the box to keep the eggs from rolling away from under the brooding female.
✔ Nesting material and the nest box have to be made of untreated wood.

✔ Provide a climbing aid below the entry hole on the inside of the box. This can be a small wooden ladder or a few wooden blocks.
✔ The top has to be removable or hinged so you can check the inside of the box.

Very popular are nest boxes made of a hollowed-out piece of tree trunk. They offer a better microclimate, and the natural rough surface of the interior makes it easier for the birds to climb up and down. Here, too, be sure the wood is untreated.

The Breeding Pair

For a successful mating you have to have a sexually mature and congenial pair of birds. For information on sexing cockatiels, see page 12. Although cockatiels reach sexual maturity at seven to nine months, you should wait until they are about a year old before breeding them the first time.

A pair generally stays together for life. They are quite tolerant toward other pairs and single birds. Fights arise only if a bird that already has a mate is wooed by another bird or if two pairs want to use the same nest box. To avoid these problems, keep an equal number of males and females in a communal aviary, and provide more nest boxes than pairs of birds.

Observation during Courtship

When two birds have taken a liking to each other, they sit close to each other. They can now be considered engaged, and from now on they will do almost everything together. The male also scratches the female's head and gives her kisses.

To solidify the pair bond, the male performs a courtship song in the form of a melodic and rhythmical whistling. Now and then he runs back and forth on a perch with spread wings, banging on it every so often with his beak to impress the female. Quite often he raises his

crest as he does this. Then he walks around the female with mincing steps, showing off his white wing patches, bowing to her repeatedly, and spreading his tail feathers into a fan.

Egg Laying and Brooding

The female starts laying eggs about a week after the mating has taken place. Every two days she lays an egg, eventually producing four to six eggs, occasionally more. Although both parents spend a lot of time in the box, they often don't start sitting until after the third egg. The female usually broods the eggs at night and, if necessary, during the day as well, depending on the willingness of the male to sit on the eggs.

Extensive mutual preening strengthens the pair bond.

About 18 to 21 days after the first egg appears, the chicks hatch, in the same order as the eggs were laid. The younger birds in the clutch are smaller than their siblings but generally receive the same care from the parents as the bigger ones.

Tips for Incubation

✔ The birds need quiet now. Do as little as possible in or near the nest box in order not to bother the parents. Young pairs often leave the nest if they are disturbed.

✔ If possible, wait with nest checks until no parent bird is in the box. The birds are quite protective of their brood.

✔ An even temperature of about 72°F (22°C) and a humidity of about 60 percent will contribute to good hatching results.

✔ You can check to see if the eggs are fertile by candling them with a strong light bulb. Fertile eggs show a network of blood vessels after about eight days; later, they become opaque. Infertile eggs are clear, but rotting eggs are dark, too.

✔ Don't remove infertile eggs right away, or the female may start laying more; also, these eggs often serve as support to the chicks and help keep them warm.

✔ Don't clean off dirty eggs; they are covered with a protective film.

✔ If the clutch is large and the nest box gets very dirty after a while, set the nestlings in a bowl and replace the litter in the box. But don't do this too often.

✔ Give the parent birds rearing food while they are brooding. This is a nutritious sprouted food with added animal proteins, such as hard-boiled egg, commercial egg food, or soft food for insectivorous birds.

✔ Do not give the birds food that they have never seen before. If you plan to breed the birds, get them used to rearing food before the eggs are laid. As soon as the first egg is laid, be sure to add calcium to the food. Female cockatiels easily become calcium depleted. Simply supplying a cuttlebone often is not enough because the female may be chewing it up without actually eating any of it. A calcium-depleted female is prone to egg binding.

Unplanned Brooding

Even a female kept singly can produce eggs. If this happens, do not remove the eggs

In his impressive courtship display, the male spreads his wings and tail feathers like a fan.

because the female will immediately lay more eggs to replace the ones that are gone. This puts a greater strain on the bird's system than sitting on the eggs.

If you have a pair that you don't want to breed, don't supply a nest box. If the female lays eggs all the same, leave them for the sake of the female bird, but punch a hole in both ends of the eggs with a thick needle. This will keep embryos from forming. You can also replace the eggs with artificial ones. When the female leaves the nest after a while, you can remove the eggs.

The Development of Baby Birds

Age	Weight	Appearance	Behavior
Newly hatched	About 4-5 grams	Pink skin covered with yellow down; eyes closed; feet, beak, and claws flesh-colored; lower mandible broad like a small shovel	Cannot sit or raise head; are fed an almost liquid substance
4th to 5th day	About 15 grams	Eyes begin to open	Clearly audible begging calls
10th day	About 35 grams	Eyes fully open; the first small feathers appear; first crest feathers visible on head	Can raise head and hiss softly; are being fed more and more predigested seeds; make pumping motions when begging for food
12th to 27th day	40–60 grams	Lose the egg tooth; beak has hardened; first quills break open and sometimes reveal later feather color	Recognize parents; hiss at strangers they take for enemies
28th to 35th day	About 80 grams	Feathers almost completely formed; colors somewhat fainter than in adult birds	Flap their wings in the nest box; leave the box soon after even though they cannot fly right away, having to practice first
About 35 to 40 days	80–100 grams	Plumage is complete	Begin to eat on their own; parents feed them less and less
About 6 months	80–100 grams	Molt replaces juvenile with brighter adult plumage	Completely independent
9 months	80–100 grams	Adult coloration	Sexually mature

Wing and Nail Trimming

As mentioned earlier, cockatiels are strong flyers, which is why it's important to keep your pet's wing feathers trimmed. Your avian veterinarian can show you how to trim your bird's feathers in more detail, but here's a brief overview of the process:

✔ Enlist the help of another person to hold the bird while you do the trimming. Have sharp scissors handy.

✔ Remove your bird from its cage and wrap it in a small towel. Have your assistant hold the bird on its back with the thumb and middle finger on either side of the bird's head and the index finger on top of the bird's head.

✔ Gently unfold one wing from the bird's side and look at the feathers. You want to trim the long flight feathers on the end of the bird's wing as closely as you can to the next row of feathers above it on the wing (this is easier to see if you look at the bird right side-up).

Trim the long flight feathers (called *primaries*) as close as you can to the end of the next row (called the *secondaries*) without cutting the bird's skin or injuring its wing. If you see dark-colored feathers that look like they're wrapped in plastic, don't cut them. They are called blood feathers and need to finish growing in before you cut them.

✔ Trim each primary feather individually. Repeat the process on the other wing. Allow your assistant to let the bird out of the towel. Praise it and tell it how good it was during the clipping so it will associate grooming with the praise.

Nail clipping on cockatiels is pretty straightforward. With the bird wrapped in a small towel, expose one of its feet. Clip or file each nail so that you remove only the hooked portion. Do this gradually to minimize bleeding, and apply cornstarch and direct pressure if you cut too deeply.

The Bird Bath

Most cockatiels enjoy taking a bath in the form of a shower. They spread their wings so that the water can reach all parts of the body. Birds will often hang upside down from the roof of the cage or aviary in order to catch every drop of water from above. Baths enhance the birds' well-being, give them something to do, and stimulate the preening impulse. Give your cockatiel the chance to bathe as often as possible, particularly in winter, when the birds suffer from the dry air of our heated houses.

Baths should be given during the day, preferably in the morning, to give the bird enough time to dry off and put its feathers back in order.

Feeling your cockatiel's claws when it's on your shoulder tells you it may need a nail trim.

Warm water from a spray bottle is a substitute for rain.

This is what the feathers of a well-groomed cockatiel look like.

Never get a bird wet and then turn off the light in the room. You can imitate the natural summer rain by using a spray bottle or mister sold for watering plants. But be sure no trace of chemicals is in the bottle. Fill the bottle with hot water from the tap and set the valve on very fine. The spray coming from the valve will be hand-warm. Now spray the bird from all sides. Do not spray the bird with anything other than water; chemicals can irritate the skin.

A cockatiel usually performs its own pedicure.

The Bathhouse

If your bird likes to take a tub bath, perhaps in a relatively wide clay bowl that is not too deep or in a bathhouse for parrots sold at pet stores, it can decide for itself when to bathe. Some birds also like to take baths in a bowl with wet leaves. Just make sure the leaves come from unsprayed trees.

Not all cockatiels take to a bathhouse; some prefer showers.

BEHAVIOR AND ACTIVITIES

Cockatiels have been living in captivity for a long time and are considered domesticated. They have retained a number of behavior patterns from their natural state that you should know about to help you understand your bird and keep it well occupied.

The Curious Cockatiel

There is hardly a creature as curious about everything around it as a tame cockatiel. Anything that looks at all interesting, makes the slightest noise, or is attractive for some other reason is checked out and investigated thoroughly. This makes sense in the cockatiel's Australian homeland, where the birds have to pay attention to the changing conditions of their environment and adjust to them. In your home, this natural behavior can give rise to comical situations but also put the bird in real danger.

✔ If you flush the toilet in the bird's presence, it will watch intently, trying to figure out where the water comes from. Should it bend too far over the rim of the bowl it could slip in and possibly drown—if you are not there watching.

✔ After a thorough visual inspection, the bird will explore any new object with the beak and the tongue. This can have disastrous effects if the object is a hot iron or contains poisonous substances.

Once a pair bond has formed, the two birds will do everything together.

✔ If certain things happen repeatedly in a certain way, the cockatiel will quickly grasp the principle involved. Thus, a bird will not take long to figure out how and through what opening it leaves the cage. If the cage door is locked it will patiently investigate the lock, and if the lock isn't too tricky the bird may figure out how to undo it and decide to take a spin in the room on its own. If the window happens to be open, there is, of course, a special danger of escape.

Typical Activities

Preening

Preening is one of the most important activities for birds in the wild, for only a plumage in prime condition protects against inclement weather and allows quick escape from predators. Birds in captivity, too, preen themselves several times a day. A cockatiel can easily spend two to three hours, but with interruptions, cleaning, sorting, and rearranging its feathers. Each feather is drawn through the beak to free it of dust and dirt and smooth it. Then oil and powder are applied to make the plumage waterproof. That is why birds can fly in the rain without getting soaked and cold. The oil is produced in a special gland just above the base of the tail, called the *uropygial* or oil gland. The bird picks up the oily secretion with its beak and distributes it evenly over the plumage. The head, which is out of the beak's reach, is rubbed directly over the gland. The powder comes from "powder down."

Scratching

Scratching is another normal daily activity. It serves the purpose of removing particles of dirt and relieving itches. If your bird keeps scratching the same spot a lot, you should consult the veterinarian to find out the reason. Perhaps your bird has parasites. Cockatiels scratch their heads by raising the foot under the wing.

Shaking the Feathers

Shaking the feathers is something you will see your cockatiel do several times a day, especially in the morning. A shaking motion runs along the whole body, often producing a rustling sound. Shaking serves, first of all, to get rid of dust and, secondly, to get all the feathers to lie where they belong, so that the plumage is in top condition for quick takeoff, if necessary. Birds will also shake themselves to relieve tension after an exciting or upsetting experience.

Fluffing

A brief fluffing of the mask, that is, a raising of the head feathers, may be a reaction to an unfamiliar event, or if the bird is mildly irritated, such as by a noise or an annoying light. Cockatiels are able to fluff up or raise just these feathers. Young birds, especially, look cute when they do this because it makes the head look even rounder than usual. Adult birds as well as juveniles raise the head feathers shortly before going to sleep or while dozing.

Cockatiels display true acrobatics to get at food they like.

When the bird fluffs its entire plumage, all the feathers of the body stand up. They no longer hug the body and, instead, create a kind of insulating air cushion. Cockatiels fluff themselves up primarily when they are cold, but sometimes also for sleeping. If a bird sits in one place all day with puffed-up feathers when it is not particularly cold, this is a sign of possible illness that should not be ignored. Such a bird will often rest on both legs instead of on just one, out of weakness.

Beak Whetting

Beak whetting is always done after a meal but sometimes at other times of day as well.

The bird rubs its beak against a cage bar or, preferably, against a branch or twig. Natural branches are best for this. Beak whetting serves to remove bits of leftover food, especially fruit and egg food, that tends to stick to the beak. The bird may also whet its beak in situations it perceives as difficult or threatening. This apparently irrelevant reaction, called a *displacement activity*, may diffuse anxiety associated with a particular situation. The physical purpose is to smooth out minor irregularities in the beak surface.

Whetting the beak can also be a form of greeting, as, for example, when you return after a prolonged absence. By making similar motions against a branch with your fingernail, you can approximate the response another cockatiel would make to this gesture.

Eating is one way for a cockatiel to keep busy.

Yawning

Yawning is something all parrots do. They generally yawn when a lack of oxygen makes them feel sleepy. Birds that are kept indoors are very sensitive to stale air. If you see your cockatiel yawning during the day, air the room thoroughly.

Sneezing

A cockatiel's sneezing is like our nose blowing, a way to clear the nasal passages. This type of sneezing often occurs during preening. Sneezing can also indicate a sinus infection. While cockatiels rarely get a "runny nose," a sinus infection is usually accompanied by reddened, enlarged nostrils.

UNDERSTANDING
BEHAVIOR

In order to understand your cockatiel's language you have to be able to interpret its behavior accurately.

 This is what my cockatiel does.

? *What is it expressing by doing this?*

! *How do I respond to its behavior?*

The bird is pulling a feather through its beak.

? It is cleaning and smoothing the feather.

! If no feathers are pulled out, leave the bird alone.

These two cockatiels are screaming at each other.

They are engaged in a quarrel.

If the quarrel turns into a serious fight, you have to intervene and separate the birds.

This cockatiel is scratching its head.

It is preening itself.

If the bird is not scratching only one spot, this is part of the daily routine.

This bird is stretching one wing and one leg.

? It has finished one activity, such as preening.

! Devote some time to your bird now; it is feeling relaxed.

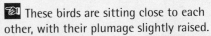 These birds are sitting close to each other, with their plumage slightly raised.

❓ They want to take a nap together.

❗ Please, don't disturb for a while.

One bird is 👈 scratching the other's neck.

This is how ❓ cockatiels express their affection for each other.

Watch the ❗ pair. If it seems indicated, make a nest box available.

👈 Two birds are preening at the same time.

❓ This social behavior suggests that they are a mated pair.

❗ Enjoy watching their interactions without disturbing the birds.

👈 This bird is shaking itself with a rustling noise.

❓ It is getting the feathers to lie in their proper place.

❗ Now it is ready for action. Play with it.

👈 This cockatiel is raising its wings.

❓ It is stretching its muscles.

❗ Offer it an opportunity to fly.

Movements and Postures

You will often observe the following movements in your cockatiel:

✔ Stretching the legs is a typical movement, in which one leg together with the wing of the same side is stretched backward and then returned to normal position. The toes are curled up during the stretch. This movement is comparable to our stretching. It relaxes tired leg muscles and other parts of the body.

✔ Tucking the beak in the back feathers is another typical gesture. Cockatiels sleep in this position if they feel safe. The head is rotated 180 degrees, and the beak is buried in the slightly fluffed-up back feathers.

✔ Birds also swivel their heads a full 180 degrees when they preen the feathers of the back.

✔ Resting on one leg serves to take the weight off the other leg and relax it. Birds often sleep standing on one leg, and they often rest during the day by pulling one leg up. Birds kept in an outdoor aviary also pull up one leg at a time to keep warm when the weather gets cold. Cockatiels missing one leg should therefore not be kept outdoors in the winter.

✔ Cockatiels look especially comical when they stretch a leg backward and then bring it forward with a theatrical flourish to tuck it into the abdominal feathers.

✔ Raising both wings simultaneously is another exercise that serves as relaxation. Your bird will also raise its wings when it is very hot in order to release body heat. The same behavior is displayed in a very different situation, namely, during a luxurious shower when the bird tries to expose as much of its body as possible to the water. Spreading both wings sideways is part of the male's courtship display behavior (see page 36). It is meant to impress the chosen female and arouse her admiration. The head is lowered, the body kept erect at a steep angle, and the tail pointed upward. If your cockatiel has

become imprinted to humans, it may woo you by assuming this posture. Take it as a compliment.

The completely erect crest is a sign of the male's excitement as it woos the female.

Sensory Perceptions

Vision

Vision is the most highly developed sense of cockatiels. In captivity, as in nature,

What the Crest Tells You

Position of the Crest	What Does It Mean?
The crest lies almost flat on the head with the tip pointing slightly upward. The plumage is completely smooth.	The bird is calm and relaxed.
The crest is raised vertically.	The bird is busy with something that absorbs its attention. It is interested, perhaps investigating some new object.
The crest is raised as far as it will go, almost pointing forward.	This is a sign of great excitement and tension, as well as of concentration.
The cockatiel snaps its crest back and hisses; the head is stretched forward.	The bird is anxious and insecure; it is afraid of something.

cockatiels feel most secure when they can survey their surroundings from an elevated perch so that they can detect a potential enemy in good time to hide or flee. That is why a cage should never be placed low.

Cockatiels initially respond to anything new in their surroundings with skepticism, but after a while, this often gives way to curiosity. Any new object is watched closely before it is accepted so it is better not to make changes in the bird's surroundings during the acclimation phase. The same applies to the clothing you wear.

The perception of color is quite highly developed in birds because color plays such an important role in their natural environment: in the wooing of a mate, the search for food, and the recognition of predators. As in many animals, the eyes are placed on the side of the head for panoramic vision; consequently, cockatiels can see what is happening behind their backs.

In order not to miss anything in their rapid flight, birds have the ability to register and process about five times as many images per second as humans.

Hearing

The sense of hearing is also well developed. Cockatiels need to hear well to be able to communicate with each other in nature across long distances. The range of sounds they hear is almost the same as for humans. Sounds a cockatiel hears often and that are therefore familiar don't arouse its attention, but unfamiliar ones can scare a bird even if they are not at all loud. Classical music seems to be soothing if played softly. The vacuum cleaner, on the other hand, may elicit cries of displeasure.

Taste

The sense of taste is not very important for birds living in the wild. Birds learn what is suitable for eating from their parents. Individual

experience can also play a role. The selection of available food is, of course, not great enough in the cockatiels' homeland for the birds to be very selective. Wild cockatiels usually check food out with their tongue and spit out what is inedible before they really taste it.

Birds in captivity can be quite finicky about what they eat and may test your patience with their determination to eat only what they like. Apparently almost all cage birds like salt. You can therefore include a piece of pretzel now and then in the menu. But caution is in order: Too much salt is bad for the kidneys. In the wild, birds satisfy their need for salt by eating earth and plants containing minerals.

The position of the crest indicates that this bird is examining the contents of the basket with great concentration.

Smell

We know very little about the sense of smell in birds, but it seems likely that birds perceive some smells, such as that of smoke and of substances with a strong, irritating odor. For this reason, if for no other, you should not smoke in the vicinity of birds.

Vocalizations

If a cockatiel feels threatened, if something bothers it, or if, in the case of a male, it is performing a courtship display, it can become quite vociferous. This has earned cockatiels the reputation among aviculturists of being very noisy. In fact, cockatiels are unpleasantly loud only in certain situations or if kept singly. Most of the time cockatiels communicate with each other and with humans in relatively quiet tones.

Cockatiels answer the calls of their fellows and respond to the words of their caretakers. The contact calls uttered in flight are quite audible and serve the cohesion of the flock. The hissing sound produced not only by adults but by young birds as well is meant to ward off enemies. But it is not particularly loud.

Screamers are usually birds that have suffered severe neglect and feel lonely and bored. If your bird is a screamer you should review its living conditions. Another possibility is to get a second bird as a companion.

If the bird feels happy in your home you will never consider its vocal communications with you unpleasant. A cockatiel always greets its keeper with a cry of pleasure, and when you leave the room it will give voice to disappointment.

You can try to encourage your cockatiel's vocal mimicking by saying a word or phrase repeatedly whenever a certain situation arises. For example, say "Good morning" every day when you enter the room where the bird is kept.

This bird is scrutinizing its mirror image, which it takes to be a fellow cockatiel.

TIP

Fun Observations

A new toy will be eyed suspiciously when it is first introduced. Watch the position of the cockatiel's crest as the bird gets acquainted with the new object. Quite often the first response will be hissing. But once the bird realizes that the toy is harmless it will investigate it, nibbling on it and feeling it with the tongue. While thus occupied, it almost forgets the world around it and will occasionally emit soft squeaking sounds.

The cockatiel will react similarly to changes in the room where it is allowed to fly. Such changes introduce variety into the daily routine, but don't overdo it. The bird can become stressed if it must constantly adjust to innovations.

Play

To keep a cockatiel's mental capabilities from deteriorating, make it a point to interact a lot with your one bird. If you don't have the time, supply toys to introduce some variety into the bird's life.

Wooden toys such as rings, ladders, or spools strung on some rope are very popular.

Mirrors give the bird the impression that there is another bird present. Mirrors made of glass break easily, so you should choose a metal one. A metal mirror can also be used by the bird to make noise.

Small cowbells also make charming toys for cockatiels. Avoid jingle-type bells because they can trap a bird's toe or tongue.

Cardboard boxes and toilet paper rolls provide no-cost entertainment. Cut the side of the toilet paper roll before giving it to your bird so it can escape easily if the roll gets stuck on its head.

✔ Thick strings animate the bird to do gymnastics and to use them as swings.

A ladder made of wooden rungs and sisal twine is a favorite plaything that can be utilized in all kinds of ways.

Togetherness Is Everything

When you are at home you should include your tame cockatiel in your activities.

✔ Give the bird something to occupy it while you do your housekeeping chores.

✔ When it's time to set the table, some birds like to move the silverware around for the noise it makes. On the other hand, many birds are afraid of the noisy vacuum cleaner. If this is the case with your bird, talk to it reassuringly and place it in its cage. Soon it will realize that the vacuum cleaner is harmless and may retreat to the cage on its own at the sight of the thing.

✔ If the bird does something you don't like, say *"No"* emphatically. Quite often this will stop the bird. If you are

Cockatiels are full of curiosity.

Tame cockatiels like as much physical contact with their keepers as possible.

consistent, your *"No"* eventually may be enough to keep the bird from doing things you don't approve of.

Cockatiels like to pass the time climbing and doing acrobatics.

✔ Wooden pencils get bitten to pieces. Use twigs from fruit trees to distract the bird from pencils.

✔ Climbing trees (available at pet stores) are a great success with birds. If you hang toys from the branches, the tree becomes even more interesting. The tree should have a permanent location at some distance from the cage so that the bird has to fly to it. But leave the bird in the tree only while you are in the same room.

Learning to Talk

Whistling notes or entire tunes they hear is something many cockatiels excel at. You can develop this talent in your bird by whistling the same melody for it over and over.

The ability to talk is not so impressive in cockatiels, but there are ways to bring to light a hidden talent if it exists and to further it.

1. Repeat the words you would like the bird to say as often as possible.

2. Always use the same tone of voice and the same words for a particular situation.

3. Proceed one step at a time. Let the bird learn one word or phrase; once it knows that, go on to the next word.

4. Try to eliminate distractions during the lessons.

5. The bird will concentrate best while it sits on your hand.

6. If there are times when the bird doesn't cooperate, don't lose patience and give up.

7. Don't force your cockatiel to mimic speech. If it has no gift at all in this area, enjoy its company in other ways.

Children enjoy playing with a tame bird, and the pleasure is mutual.

PREVENTIVE HEALTH CARE AND ILLNESS

Even if you offer optimal conditions, take excellent care of your bird, and provide a healthy diet, your cockatiel may, like any other creature, eventually get sick. This chapter tells you how to prevent and treat diseases and how to care for a sick bird.

An Ounce of Prevention

Preventing illness is especially important in the case of birds because they give very little sign of being sick. Remember that in the wild, a sick bird is often a dead bird, so birds naturally hide signs of illness for as long as they can. By the time you notice that something is wrong, it may already by too late.

Notice that avian illnesses are described by "signs," rather than "symptoms." Avian veterinarians use clinical signs—things that can be seen or observed—when diagnosing illnesses instead of symptoms, which are often described by human patients to their physicians.

Signs of Illness

Part of your daily care routine for your cockatiel should include observing it for signs of illness, which include the following:

- Bird has continually fluffed feathers
- Bird loses appetite
- Bird sleeps all day

Only a bird that is healthy stretches and relaxes like this.

- Bird loses weight
- Bird loses interest in surroundings
- Bird has droopy wing or lame leg
- Bird has food stuck to the face
- Bird has trouble breathing (bird's tail may bob up and down as it breathes)
- Bird has discharge from eyes or nares (nostrils)
- Bird doesn't talk or sing

If you see any of these signs of illness in your cockatiel, contact your avian veterinarian's office for an immediate appointment.

Injuries and Trauma

Injuries result from encounters with cats or other animals or from fights over nest sites or rank, as well as accidental encounters with windows, walls, or mirrors if a bird escapes from its cage.

Suspect that your bird has been injured if you see blood on the plumage and/or perch. Even if you see very little blood, examine the bird thoroughly.

Minor wounds heal by themselves. If the bleeding is heavy, try to stop it by applying gentle pressure and take the bird to the veterinarian as soon as possible.

Clean minor cuts with a water-based iodine solution. Use styptic powder only on toenails that have been trimmed too closely.

Watch your bird for signs of head injury, too, especially if it has flown into a mirror or window. These include a loss of balance, weakness in the wings or legs, unusual eye or head movements, or loss of consciousness. If you see any of these signs in your bird, contact your avian veterinarian's office for an immediate evaluation. Keep the bird as quiet as possible and transport it immediately for further treatment.

Fractures

Fractures are often caused by accidents. A broken leg or wing has to be set and splinted right away by the veterinarian to prevent the bones from fusing in the wrong position.

Skin and Plumage Diseases

If the claws and beak are growing too long, consult your avian veterinarian because your bird may have a medical problem that causes this overgrowth. If no medical issue is found, your bird may need to have routine grooming appointments at your veterinarian's office because beak trimming is best left to the professionals.

If your bird's beak is just a little overgrown, you can help keep its beak trimmed by providing a variety of chew toys for your bird in its cage. Chewing and playing help your bird keep its beak in condition, so provide several types of chew toys, and rotate them regularly to keep things interesting for your bird.

Don't use sandpaper perch covers to help keep your cockatiel's nails trimmed because these products often cause foot irritation, which can lead to infection.

If you do have to reach for the clippers, proceed with caution: cutting too far back causes bleeding. If you do happen to cut a toenail too short, apply styptic powder and direct pressure to stop the bleeding.

Malformed feathers may be genetic or the result of an inadequate diet or a metabolic disorder, but they may also be caused by viral or bacterial diseases. If you notice your bird has improperly formed feathers, contact your avian veterinarian for an appointment.

Give your bird a daily hands-on examination to check for lumps, bumps, bruises, and other signs of trouble with its feathers or skin. Report any changes to your veterinarian so he or she can identify the problem and treat it immediately.

This female is proudly displaying her long primaries.

Recognizing Signs of Illness

What You Notice	Possible Causes You Can Remedy Yourself	Additional Signs Requiring a Prompt Trip to the Veterinarian
Refusal to eat	Spoiled food, bird is not hungry, bird doesn't like certain foods	Diarrhea, vomiting, weight loss, permanently puffed-up plumage
Regurgitation of seeds	Courtship display behavior	Breast feathers stuck together, weight loss, sour smell, food stuck on bird's face, bird is apathetic
Trouble breathing, noisy breathing	Exhaustion after exertion, hot weather, high room temperature, high humidity, obesity	Open-mouthed breathing, rattling sound in throat, squeaking or whistling noise, tail bobbing, hanging with beak from the cage bars to get air, nasal discharge, swollen eyes
Frequent sneezing	Dry, dusty air, picking at nose with foot	Heavy discharge from nose (blood, pus), teary eyes, swollen eyes
Loose droppings	Nervousness, too much fruit in diet, stress	Frothy bubbles, bloody or abnormal color droppings, undigested food in droppings, puffed-up plumage
Unsuccessful attempts to eliminate	Minor constipation	No droppings for prolonged period, cries of pain, eggshell can be seen in vent of female bird (this is a situation called egg binding that requires veterinary attention)
Constant scratching, restlessness	Dry air, lack of bathing water	Sleeplessness, apathy, feather pulling, self-mutilation, skin infection
Limping, favoring one leg/wing	Bruising, pulled muscle or ligament	Leg or wing hanging down limply, bird can't put weight on leg, open wounds, broken bone

Intestinal Tract Diseases

A cockatiel uses not only its feet but also its beak to hold on.

The droppings of birds are made up of feces (greenish brown), uric acid (white), and urine (clear liquid). If the white part is watery, it may indicate kidney problems. Watery droppings can also be caused by a diet high in fruits, so your veterinarian may recommend that you withhold fruits and vegetables for two days to determine the cause of your bird's loose droppings.

In the case of diarrhea, the greenish brown part of the dropping is runny, and the feathers near the vent are soiled. The droppings may be bloody, and the bird may sit around apathetically. Many possible causes—including spoiled food, ingestion of poisonous substances, and bacteria—exist for diarrhea. In order for the disease not to spread, you should separate the affected bird and keep it under a red heat lamp until you can get it to the veterinarian.

Causes of constipation include inappropriate diet, ingestion of foreign objects, a tumor or swelling that closes off the vent, egg binding, or lack of exercise. Have the veterinarian determine the cause and prescribe treatment.

Crop inflammation prevents proper digestion of food. The first signs are sneezing, vomiting of sour-smelling crop contents, and violent head shaking. Possible causes include swallowing a foreign body, spoiled food, bacteria, or parasites. Take your bird to the veterinarian if it shows any of these signs.

Respiratory Diseases

These can range from difficult or noisy breathing to shortness of breath to pneumonia. Dry indoor air dries out the mucous membranes of the respiratory tract and makes it vulnerable to disease. Problems can also be triggered by drafts and cigarette smoke, as well as by bacteria and fungi. Provide humidity by having a humidifier, a fountain, or an aquarium in the room.

Chlamydiosis, formerly called psittacosis or parrot fever, is a serious health threat for people as well as birds. It is a bacterial infection manifested by nasal discharge, conjunctivitis, and apathetic behavior. An affected cockatiel will sit with its plumage permanently puffed up, and its droppings may be bright green. People suffering from the disease develop flulike symptoms. Immediate medical attention is crucial for the recovery of both birds and people.

Visiting the Veterinarian

A healthy cockatiel should be seen for an annual checkup by an avian veterinarian; if your bird has other health issues, it may need to be seen more frequently. If you notice a change in your bird's appearance or behavior, consult your veterinarian.

Find out before an emergency arises where there is a second veterinarian (in case your regular one is unavailable) or if there is an emergency clinic.

If you can, take your bird to the veterinarian in its normal cage so the doctor can evaluate the cage setup. If this isn't possible, transport your bird in a travel carrier.

Questions Your Veterinarian May Ask

1. *Ownership*: How old is the bird? How long have you owned it? Where did you get it?
2. *Current Health*: What are the droppings like? (You may want to take a sample.) When did you first notice a change? What struck you in particular? Has the cockatiel had similar or other clinical signs or diseases in the past? Has it been treated before and, if so, for how long and with what medication?
3. *Daily Care*: What do you feed the bird? What does it drink? When did it last eat fresh food and what kind? Has there been a recent change in its diet?
4. *Environment*: Does the bird have contact with any hazardous materials, such as paint, lead weights in the drapes, and so on? Do you have other birds or pets? Where is the cage located? Have any people the bird is in contact with gotten sick?

A sick bird will often sleep crouching on the ground.

Note: You can tell that a bird is sick if it sits apathetically in a corner or on a perch with dull, glassy eyes.

Quarantine

If you keep several cockatiels and one of them comes down with a contagious disease, the sick bird should be segregated. Put it in a separate cage or a so-called "sick box," a cage that can be heated. If you have just one bird you can leave it in its regular cage.

The cage with the sick bird should be in a quiet, dry room with a temperature of 72–76°F (22 to 24°C). Avoid anything that might cause excitement or stress.

Giving Medication

Be sure to follow the veteri-narian's directions concerning dosage. This is especially important if the medication has to be continued over some time. If you stop giving it too soon, the bird may suffer a relapse.

Sick birds can receive medication by injection, by mouth, or by topical application to the skin. Ask your avian veterinarian to demonstrate the method by which your bird will be treated so that you understand completely what you need to do to help your bird get well.

Injection

To give your bird an injection, have an assistant catch the bird in a small towel. The assistant should hold the bird's head by placing the thumb on one side of the head and the middle finger on the other

Giving Medication Directly into the Beak

With a very weakened bird that doesn't eat or drink on its own, medication has to be given directly into the beak. Hold the bird loosely in a towel, then introduce the medication slowly into the beak toward the right side of the throat with a disposable syringe. Give the bird time to swallow between doses.

side. The index finger can be used to scratch the bird's head in an effort to calm it during toweling.

Insert the needle into the bird's chest muscle at a 45-degree angle and administer the medication. Remember to alternate injection sites while medicating your bird so that one spot on its chest doesn't become overly sore. You can either alternate left and right, or you can consider the bird's chest as a clock face and start your medication routine at 12 o'clock and work around the chest.

Applying Ointments

Immobilize the bird with a towel and have another person dab the ointment on the required spot with a cotton swab.

The best way to give a bird medicine is with a syringe.

Using a Heat Lamp

A heat lamp speeds recovery.

✔ Mount the lamp in such a way that the rays feel comfortable on your hand held at the same distance from the lamp as the bird will be.

✔ Water always has to be available.

✔ Keep the lamp on constantly.

✔ At night, darken the cage half that is not exposed to the rays with a cloth.

✔ When your cockatiel begins to feel better, turn the lamp off periodically at shorter and shorter intervals. The temperature in the room should drop only slowly.

Expose only half the cage to the heat lamp so that the bird can move to a cooler spot.

Disinfecting

In case of a contagious disease or after the successful conclusion of treatment, all the objects the patient had any contact with should be disinfected. Ask your veterinarian to recommend an appropriate product.

Helping Your Bird Regain Strength

Once an illness has been overcome, you should do everything you can to nurse your bird back to its former physical condition. Healthy and varied food, plenty of fresh air, and devoting special attention to the recuperating patient will achieve a great deal. Giving extra vitamins will enhance natural resistance.

Emergency Kit

✔ Towels to catch and hold the bird

✔ Address and telephone number of your veterinarian and the nearest avian emergency clinic

✔ Nail trimmers

✔ Water-based iodine solution

✔ Styptic powder (for stopping bleeding on nails)

✔ Cornstarch (for stopping bleeding on feathers or skin)

✔ Cotton swabs

✔ Saline solution or other eye wash

✔ Energy supplement, such as Pedialyte or glucose

✔ Eyedropper

✔ Syringes

✔ Small flashlight

✔ Small, blunt-tipped scissors

✔ Needle-nosed pliers

✔ Blunt-tipped tweezers

✔ Magnifying glass

✔ Gauze squares, gauze rolls, and masking tape for bandages

✔ Stretch bandage

Store these items in a tackle box or backpack near your bird's cage.

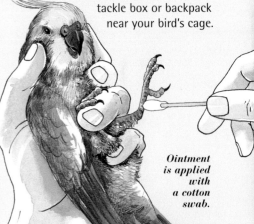

Ointment is applied with a cotton swab.

I N D E X

Organizations

American Cockatiel Society Inc. (ACS)
11152 Blackwood Drive
New Port Richey, FL 34654
www.acstiels.com

   The ACS was founded to encourage an interest in and an understanding of the cockatiel as a pet, breeder, or show bird. The ACS hosts shows around the United States and publishes a quarterly magazine for its members.

National Cockatiel Society (NCS)
140 Almy Street
Warwick, RI 02886
www.cockatiels.org

   The NCS is a nonprofit organization that provides information on proper care, handling, maintenance, and breeding of cockatiels. The NCS hosts shows around the United States and publishes a bimonthly magazine for its members.

Books

Grindol, Diane. *Cockatiels for Dummies.* Indianapolis, IN: *For Dummies Books*, 2001.

——. *The Complete Book of Cockatiels.* New York, NY: Howell Book House, 1998.

Higdon, Pamela. *The Essential Cockatiel.* New York, NY: Howell Book House, 1999.

Mancini, Julie. *Your Happy Healthy Pet: Cockatiel.* Hoboken, NJ: Wiley Publishing/Howell Book House, 2006.

Moustaki, Nikki. *Why Do Cockatiels Do That? Real Answers to the Curious Things Cockatiels Do.* Irvine, CA: Bowtie Press, 2003.

Important Note

   People allergic to feathers or feather dust should not keep birds. Consult your doctor before getting one.

   Chlamydiosis is a bacterial infection that people can contract if they come in contact with the nasal secretion or inhale dust particles from the droppings of infected birds (see page 57). If you think your cockatiel might have chlamydiosis, have the veterinarian check it out, and if you have cold or flu symptoms, see your doctor and tell him or her that you keep birds.

Acknowledgments

The authors wish to express gratitude to their parents, who always actively supported their interests, and to their families, who enabled them to find the time to work on this book.

The photographer wants to thank Karl Gerbl and Sepp Christ for lending her their birds so she could take pictures of them; also Regina Wolf, Monika Dressel, and Birgit Kuhl and son Lukas for allowing her to photograph their cockatiels.

About the Authors

Thomas Haupt grew up with animals and has been a practicing veterinarian since 1992. A fairly large proportion of his patients are birds. He keeps a number of birds himself, especially parrots of various species. Dr. Haupt also maintains an infirmary for injured wild animals.

Pet birds have been an important part of Julie Mancini's life since she was a child. Her first pet was a parakeet, and she cared for an African grey with special needs for more than 10 years. A former editor of *Bird Talk*, Julie has been a freelance writer for the past 12 years. She and her family currently live on a small acreage in south-central Iowa, where they plan to raise goats, sheep, and alpacas.

About the Photographer

Karin Skogstad has been working as a freelance journalist and photographer since 1979, specializing in animals and plants.

The Artist

György Jankovics is a trained graphic artist and has studied at the art academies of Budapest and Hamburg. He does animal and plant illustrations for a number of major publishing houses.

English translation © Copyright 2008, 1999 by Barron's Educational Series, Inc.

Original title of the book in German is *Nymphensittiche*.

Translated from the German by Rita Kimber.

Copyright © 1998 by Gräfe und Unzer Verlag GmbH, Munich.

G|U

All inquiries should be addressed to:
Barron's Educational Series, Inc.
250 Wireless Boulevard
Hauppauge, New York 11788
www.barronseduc.com

Library of Congress Catalog Card No. 2007034602

ISBN–13: 978-0-7641-3896-6
ISBN–10: 0-7641-3896-0

Library of Congress Cataloging-in-Publication Data
Haupt, Thomas.
    [Nymphensittiche. English]
    Cockatiels : everything about purchase, care, behavior, and health / Thomas Haupt and Julie Rach Mancini ; illustrations by György Jankovics ; [translated from the German by Rita Kimber]. — 2nd ed.
        p. cm.
    Includes index.
    ISBN–13: 978-0-7641-3896-6
    ISBN–10: 0-7641-3896-0
    1. Cockatiel. I. Mancini, Julie R. (Julie Rach) II. Title.

SF473.C6H38513   2008
636.6′8656—dc22   2007034602

Printed in China

9 8 7 6 5 4

EXPERT ADVICE

An expert answers the ten most frequently asked questions about keeping cockatiels as pets.

1 Should I keep just one or at least two cockatiels?

2 Do birds of the same sex get along?

3 Do I have to have my landlord's permission to keep birds?

4 Is it better to buy from a breeder or a pet store?

5 Where can I get a specific color strain?

6 Are cockatiels expensive?

7 What should I watch for especially when buying a cockatiel?

8 Can cockatiels be house-trained?

9 Can cockatiels injure a human and can they represent a health hazard for humans?

10 Can cockatiels be given scraps from the table?